★
THE
BIG
TIME

STEPHEN CURRY

LAURA K. MURRAY

CREATIVE EDUCATION CREATIVE PAPERBACKS

STEPHEN CURRY

TABLE OF CONTENTS

MEET STEPHEN

Stephen dribbles down the court. He weaves between defenders. The crowd chants, "Steph! Steph! Steph!" Stephen stops and takes a shot. The ball soars high and long. *Swish!*

Stephen (*STEFF-in*) Curry is a point guard for the Golden State Warriors. The team is part of the National Basketball Association (NBA). Many people think Stephen is one of the best players today!

Stephen is 6-foot-3 and weighs 190 pounds.

STEPHEN'S CHILDHOOD

Stephen was born March 14, 1988, in Akron, Ohio. He grew up in North Carolina. His parents were great athletes. His dad, Dell, played in the NBA! Stephen has two siblings. His brother Seth plays pro basketball, too.

Dell played for the Charlotte Hornets.

AKRON, OHIO

GETTING INTO BASKETBALL

Stephen always liked basketball. He was a star on his high school team. But many people thought he was too small. Big colleges did not offer him a place on their teams.

....

Stephen with his dad at the 1992 NBA Three-Point Contest.

Stephen went to Davidson College in North Carolina. Stephen became the school's all-time leading scorer. He had the most three-pointers and free throws, too. He averaged 25.3 points, 4.5 rebounds, and 3.7 assists per game.

In 2008, Stephen topped all college basketball players in scoring.

THE BIG TIME

Stephen left college early to play pro basketball. The Golden State Warriors *drafted* him in 2009. So he moved to California. He made 166 three-pointers as a *rookie*. In 2010–11, Stephen's free throw percentage (.934) set a Warriors record.

Stephen set an NBA record with 402 three-pointers in the 2015–16 season.

The next season, Stephen was hurt and missed many games. But he came back ready to play. He and teammate Klay Thompson scored lots of points together. People called them the "Splash Brothers." They sent balls splashing through the net!

The "Splash Brothers" team up to block a player.

OFF THE COURT

Stephen likes spending time with his family. He and his wife, Ayesha, have two daughters. Stephen also enjoys golf. He hosts **charity** golf tournaments. Stephen's **faith** is very important to him.

....

Stephen with his wife, Ayesha, and daughter Riley in 2015.

WHAT IS NEXT?

Stephen was named the league's Most Valuable Player in 2015 and 2016. He helped the Warriors win the 2015 NBA championship! The Warriors lost the Finals in 2016. But they hoped to return soon!

Stephen helped the Warriors win their first title in 40 years.

WHAT STEPHEN SAYS ABOUT ...

GOOD SHOOTING FORM

"... everything is very smooth and calm from your feet through your release. Everything moves through you like a wave, almost. It's a beautiful thing."

HIS SIZE

"I have heard what people say about me ever since high school.... So I hold myself to a higher standard; it's a conscious mission to figure out ways to constantly make myself better."

MOTIVATION

"I've been blessed with talents to play this game and been put on a stage to impact a lot of people. I don't want to take that for granted. That's what drives me."

GLOSSARY

charity a group that works to help other people

drafted picked to be on a team; in a sports draft, teams take turns choosing players

faith a strong belief in God or trust in something

rookie a player in his first season

WEBSITES

Stephen Curry
http://stephencurry30.com/
This is Stephen's own website, with news, photos, and training information.

Stephen Curry Player Profile
http://www.nba.com/playerfile/stephen_curry/bio/
Read more facts and stats about Stephen.

READ MORE

Bodden, Valerie. *Kevin Durant*. Mankato, Minn.: Creative Education, 2014.

Frisch, Aaron. *LeBron James*. Mankato, Minn.: Creative Education, 2013.

INDEX

PUBLISHED BY Creative Education and Creative Paperbacks
P.O. Box 227, Mankato, Minnesota 56002
Creative Education and Creative Paperbacks
are imprints of The Creative Company
www.thecreativecompany.us

DESIGN AND PRODUCTION BY Christine Vanderbeek
ART DIRECTION BY Rita Marshall
PRINTED IN the United States of America

PHOTOGRAPHS BY Alamy (epa european pressphoto agency b.v.), Corbis (Tim Cowie/Icon SMI, Daniel Gluskoter/ICON SMI, Daniel Gluskoter/Icon Sportswire, Michael Goulding/ZUMA Press, Mark Halmas/Icon SMI, Icon SMI, Steve Lipofsky, Albert Pena/Icon SMI, Jane Tyska/ZUMA Press), Dreamstime (Ivicans), Getty Images (Andrew D. Bernstein/Contributor, Noah Graham/Contributor), iStockphoto (Pingebat), Newscom (John G. Mabanglo/EPA)

LIBRARY OF CONGRESS CATALOGING-IN-PUBLICATION DATA
Murray, Laura K.
Stephen Curry / Laura K. Murray.
p. cm. — (The big time)
Includes index.
Summary: An elementary introduction to the life, work, and popularity of Stephen Curry, a professional basketball point guard who helped the Golden State Warriors win the 2015 NBA championship.

ISBN 978-1-60818-672-3 (HARDCOVER)
ISBN 978-1-62832-268-2 (PBK)
ISBN 978-1-56660-708-7 (EBOOK)
1. Curry, Stephen, 1988–. 2. Basketball players—Biography. I. Title.
GV884.C88M87 2016
796.323092—dc23 [B]   2015026257

CCSS: RI.1.1, 2, 3, 4, 5, 6, 7; RI.2.1, 2, 5, 6, 7; RI.3.1, 5, 7, 8; RI.4.3, 5; RF.1.1, 3, 4; RF.2.3, 4

FIRST EDITION HC   9 8 7 6 5 4 3 2 1
PBK   9 8 7 6 5 4 3 2

Note: Every effort has been made to ensure that the websites listed above are suitable for children, that they have educational value, and that they contain no inappropriate material. However, because of the nature of the Internet, it is impossible to guarantee that these sites will remain active indefinitely or that their contents will not be altered.